Adam and Eve
and the
Garden
of Eden

*I have dedicated this book to the children
of Shapla Primary School.*

The Eden Project brings plants and people together.
It is dedicated to developing a greater understanding
of our shared global garden; encouraging us to
respect plants and to protect them.

THE GARDEN OF EDEN
AN EDEN PROJECT BOOK 1903 919061

Published in Great Britain by Eden Project Books,
an imprint of Transworld Publishers

This edition published 2004

1 3 5 7 9 10 8 6 4 2

Set in Bell MT

TRANSWORLD PUBLISHERS
61–63 Uxbridge Road, London W5 5SA
A division of The Random House Group Ltd

RANDOM HOUSE AUSTRALIA (PTY) LTD
20 Alfred Street, Milsons Point, Sydney,
New South Wales 2061, Australia

RANDOM HOUSE NEW ZEALAND LTD
18 Poland Road, Glenfield, Auckland 10, New Zealand

RANDOM HOUSE (PTY) LTD
Endulini, 5A Jubilee Road, Parktown 2193, South Africa

THE RANDOM HOUSE GROUP Limited Reg. No. 954009

www.**kids**at**randomhouse**.co.uk

www.edenproject.com

A CIP catalogue record for this book is available from the British Library.

Printed in Singapore

Adam and Eve

and the

Garden of Eden

Jane Ray

EDEN PROJECT BOOKS

At the very beginning of the world the earth was a dry and dusty place, where nothing could live and nothing could grow.

So God made a mist which watered the ground all over.

Then, with his great hands, he formed the first man out of the clay of the newly watered earth.

He breathed the breath of life into the man's nostrils, so that he became a warm, living soul. God gave him a name, Adam, which means "earth".

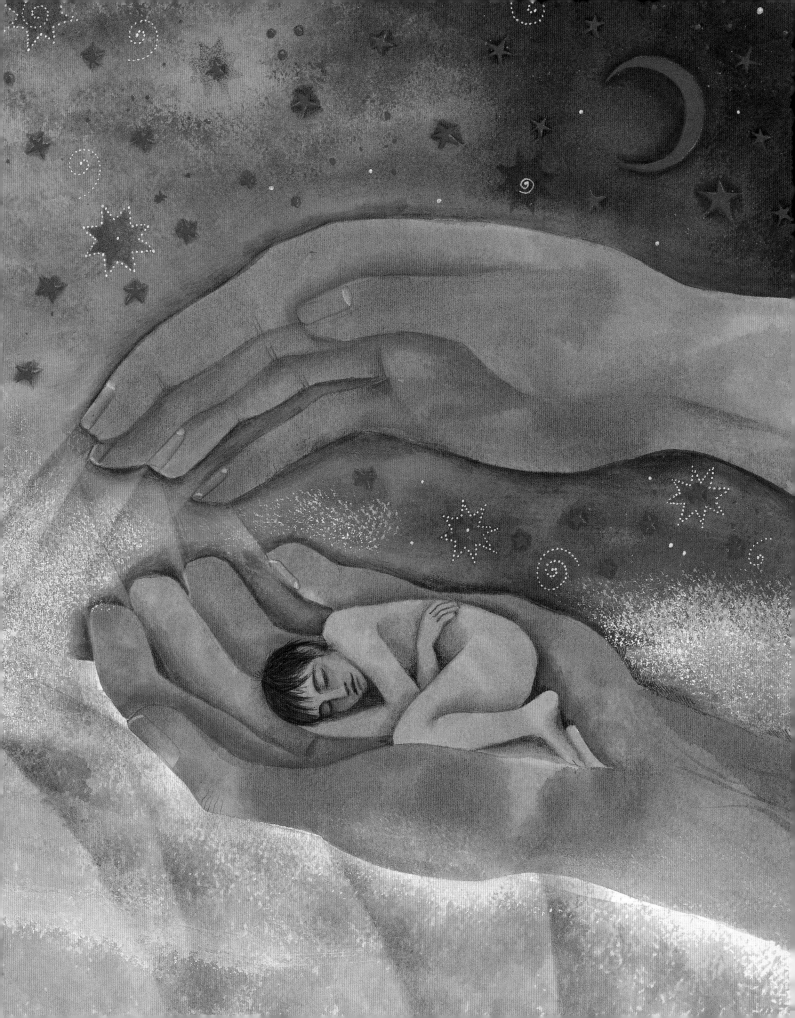

In a place called Eden, God planted a garden for Adam. It was full of plants that were beautiful to look at and good to eat.

In the middle of the
garden stood a fountain.
Two great trees grew nearby,
the Tree of Knowledge and
the Tree of Life.

God warned Adam, "You may eat anything you like except the fruits from the Tree of Knowledge and the Tree of Life. If you eat them, you will die."

The Garden of Eden was beautiful.
The scent of blossom filled the air.
Succulent fruits and berries
ripened in the sunshine.

Adam was happy to tend the
garden as God had asked him.

Adam loved his garden, but he was lonely. So God set about making creatures of every kind – the mighty and the meek, the sleek and the scaly, the spotted, feathered, dappled and striped.

Some crept,
  some slithered,
    some hopped,
      some swam,
        some flew.
Adam named them, every one. But still he needed
a friend to share his home.

So God sent
Adam into a deep
and dreaming sleep.
While Adam dreamed,
God took out one of
his ribs and closed
him up again.
God turned the rib
into a woman, the
perfect partner for
Adam. She was called
Eve, which means
"mother of all
living things".

Now Adam and Eve looked after
their magical garden together.
They lived peacefully with
the animals.

They sang and they danced and they
played – and sometimes they simply stood
quietly and gazed at the beauty of it all.
They never, ever, tasted the fruit
from the forbidden trees.

Then, one bright day, as Eve sat alone in the shade of the Tree of Knowledge, the serpent appeared beside her.

"I expect God's told you not to eat the fruit of this tree, hasn't he?" the serpent said.

Eve replied, "We can eat everything else, but if we eat the fruit from this tree, God says we'll die."

"Die? You won't die!"
The serpent crept closer
to Eve and whispered,
"The fruit from these
two trees will open
your eyes and make
you wise – like a god.
Wouldn't you like that?"

The serpent melted away into the shadows
and Eve was alone again. Eve looked at
the fruit of the Tree of Knowledge.
Would it really make her wise?

It smelled sweet.

Eve reached out her hand. The fruit was perfectly ripe.

Eve picked the fruit and bit into its juicy flesh.

When Adam came back, hot and thirsty, they ate the forbidden fruit together.

As soon as Adam and Eve
had eaten the fruit they looked
at each other, and for the first
time they felt shy.

They quickly found fig leaves
and covered themselves up.

Then they heard a voice calling them. It was God, walking in the cool of the garden. Adam and Eve felt ashamed and hid from him in the bushes.

When God saw Adam and Eve
hiding, he guessed that they
had done something wrong.
He told them to come out
from their hiding place.

God asked Adam, "Did you eat
the forbidden fruit?"
"I did," said Adam. "But it was
Eve who made me do it."
"Did you, Eve?" asked God.
"I did," said Eve. "But only because the
serpent persuaded me to."

G od was very angry.

"Because of what you have done," he said to
the serpent, "I am going to make you the most
miserable creature on earth. You will slither
everywhere on your belly, and you will
eat nothing but dust."

God turned to Adam and Eve.
"Now you will learn what it is to be sad as well as happy," he said. "You will work your fingers to the bone growing food to eat and raising your children. And when you die, you will return to the earth from which you were made."

God loved Adam
and Eve as if they were his children,
but he knew that he must send them away
from the Garden of Eden.

"Leave, before you are tempted to eat
the fruit from the Tree of Life," he said.
"You are mortal now, and cannot live
for ever."

God gave Adam and Eve warm
clothes to wear. He handed them some
seeds and cuttings from the garden.
Then he sent them out into the world.

God commanded his angels
to guard the gates of Eden. By the
Tree of Life he set a bright flame, turning
this way and that, like a sword, to protect it.

In the bare earth beyond Eden, Adam and Eve planted a new garden for their family.